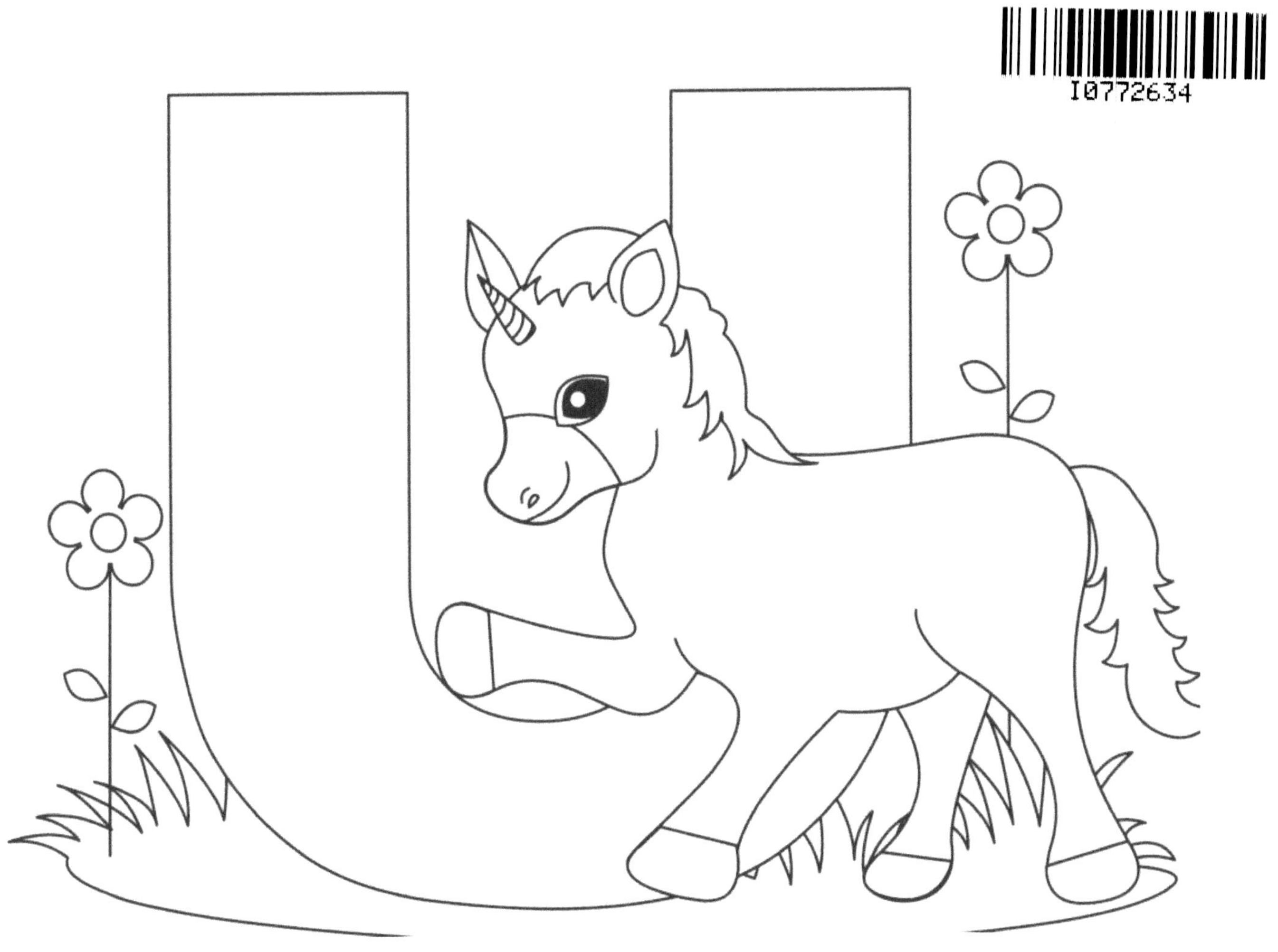

THIS BOOK BELONGS TO :

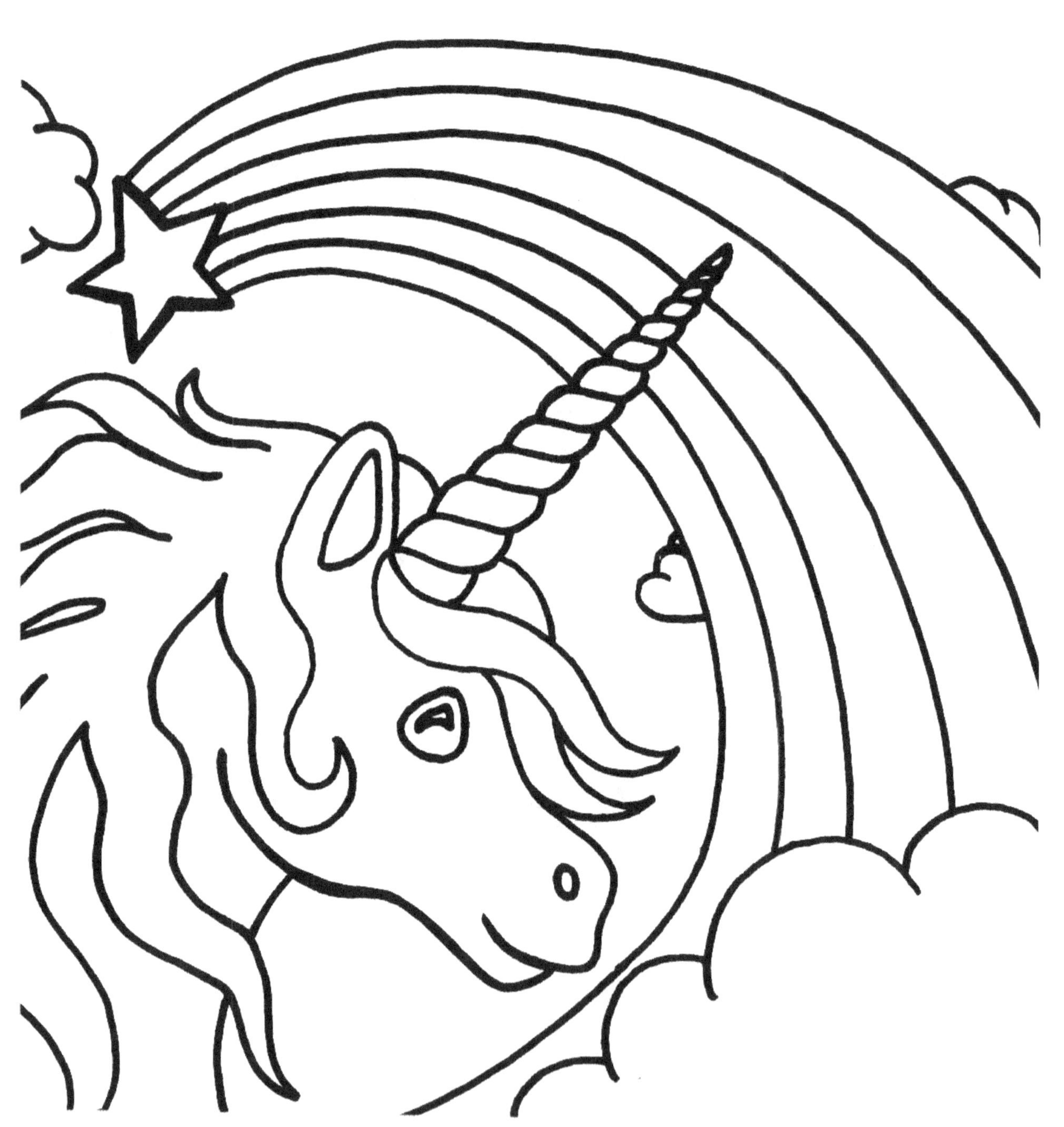

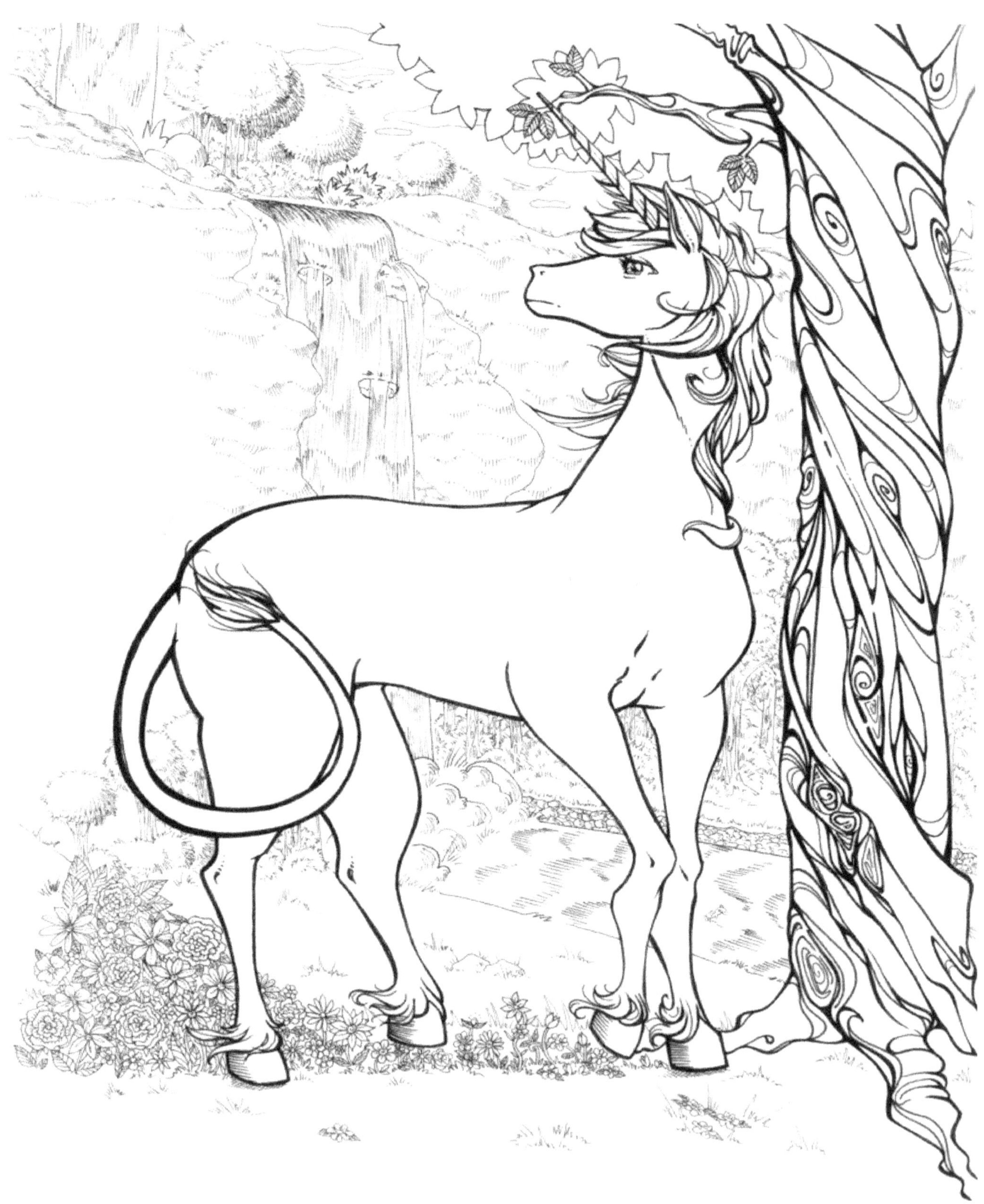

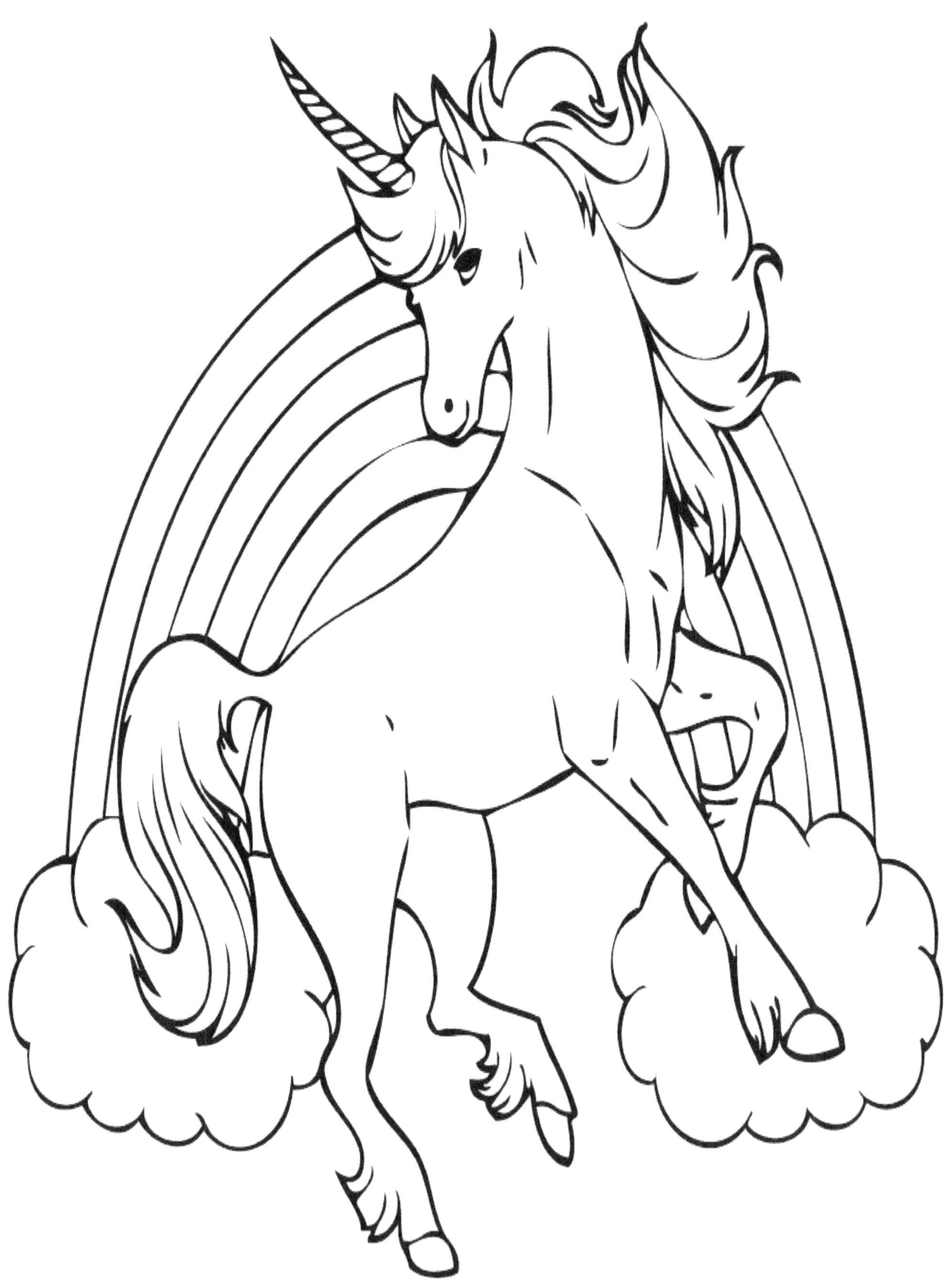

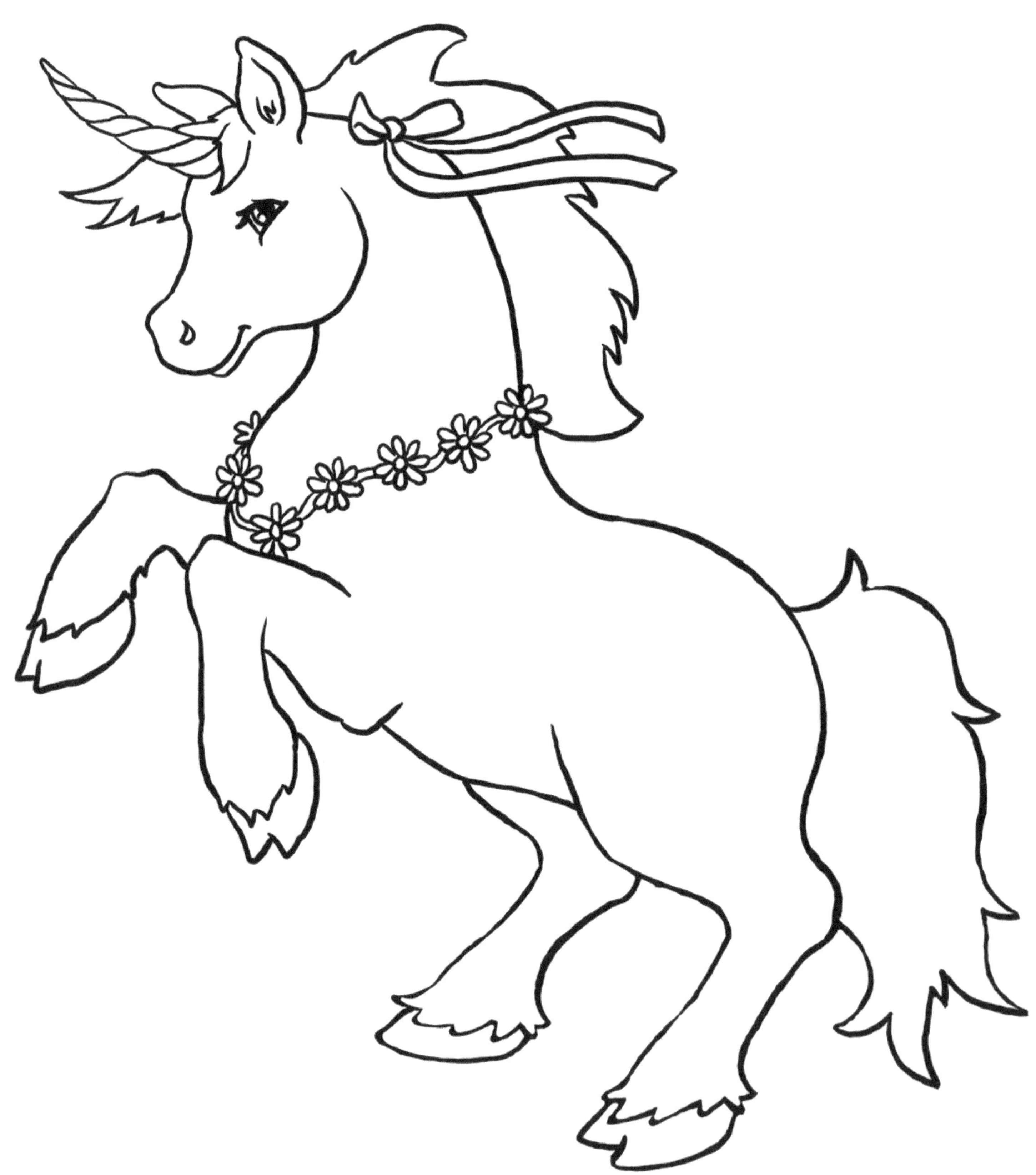

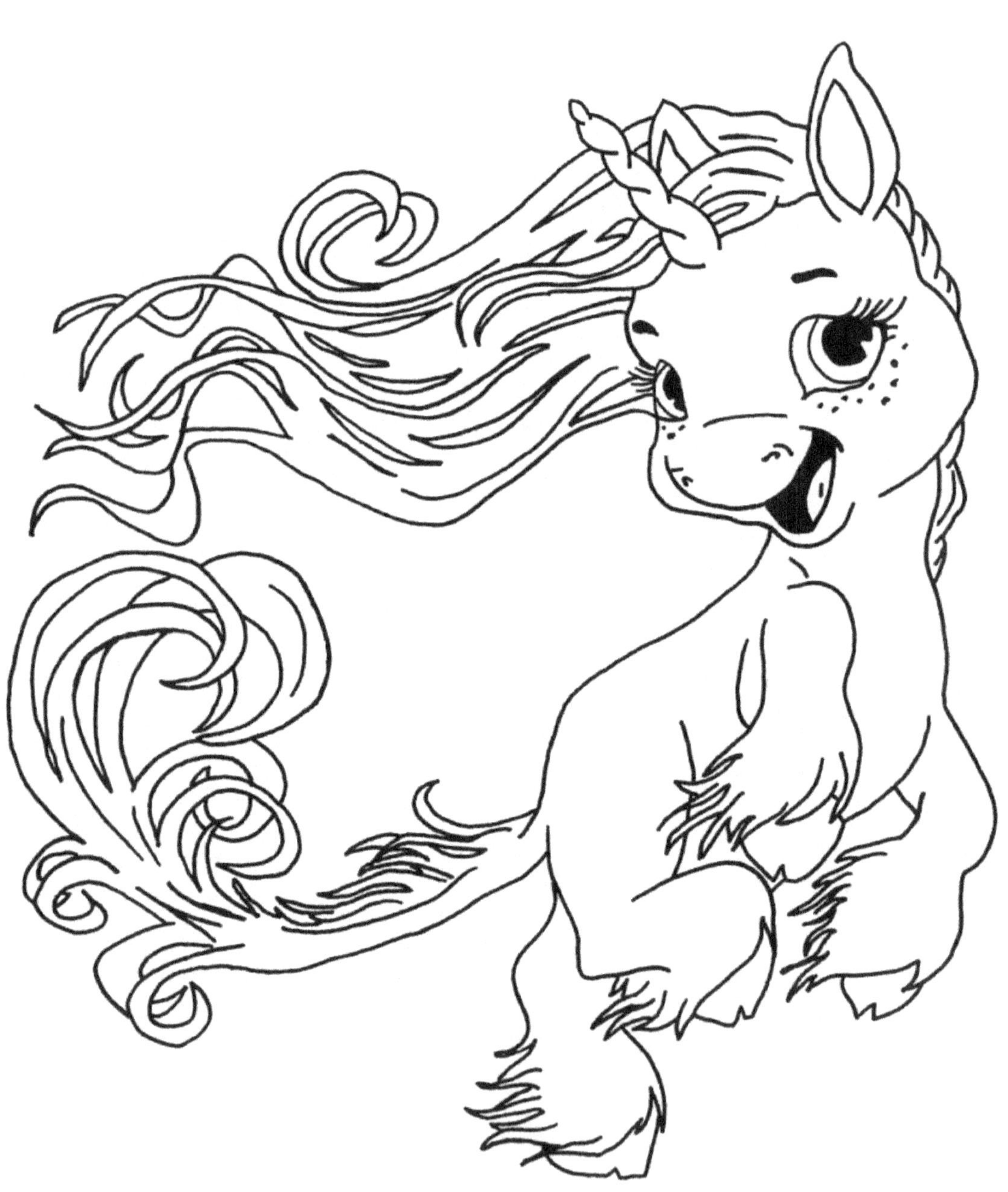

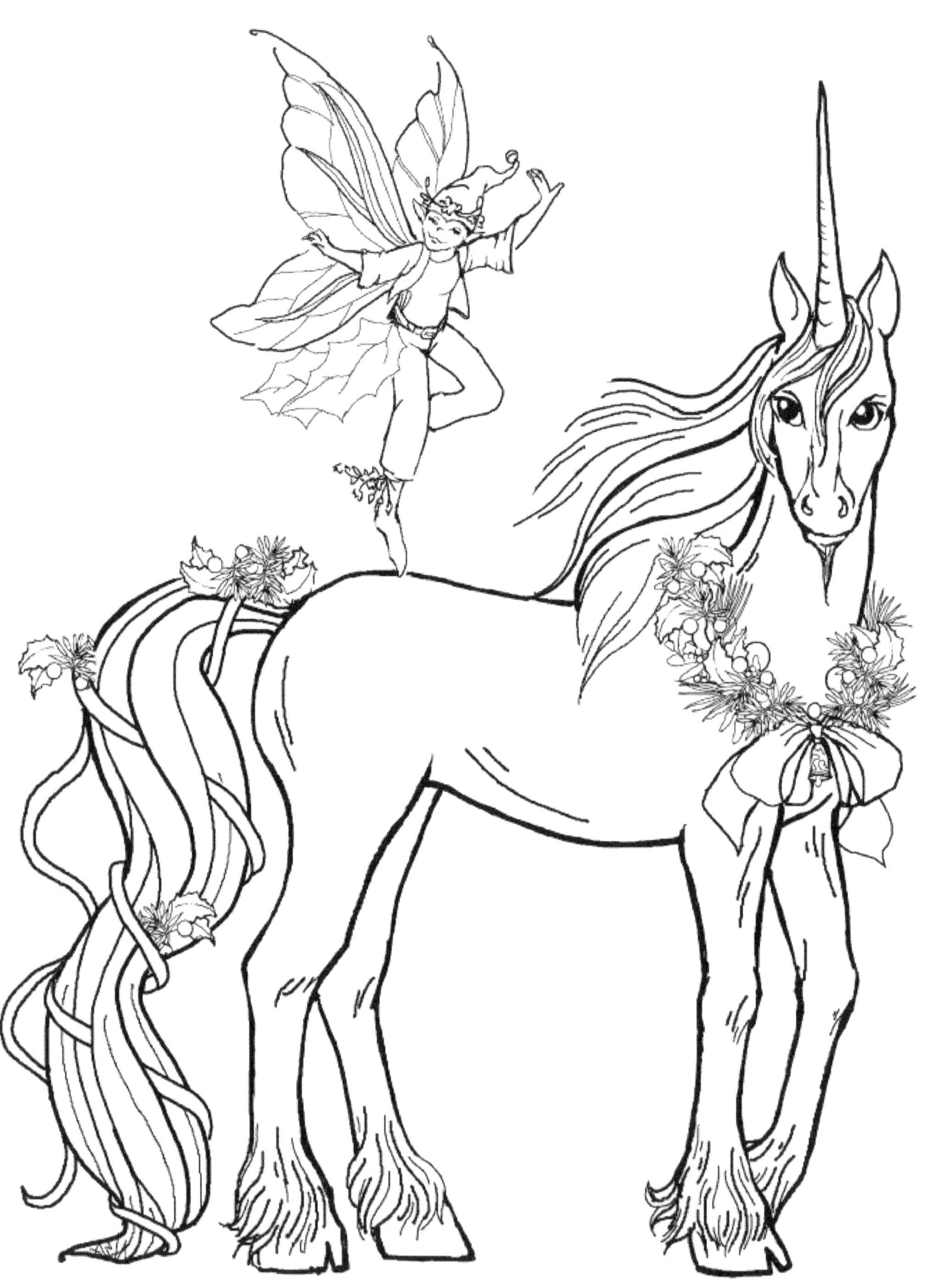

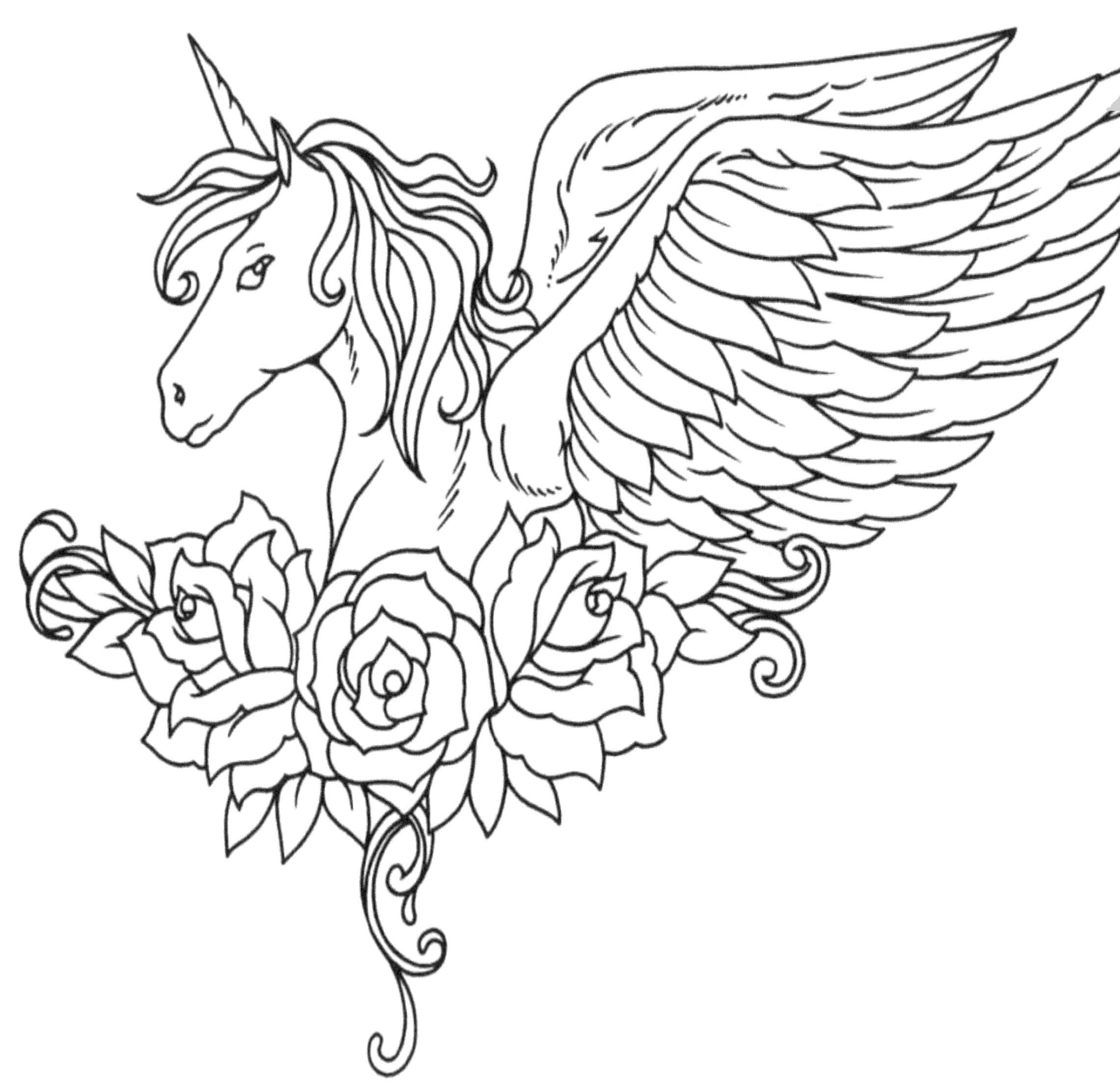

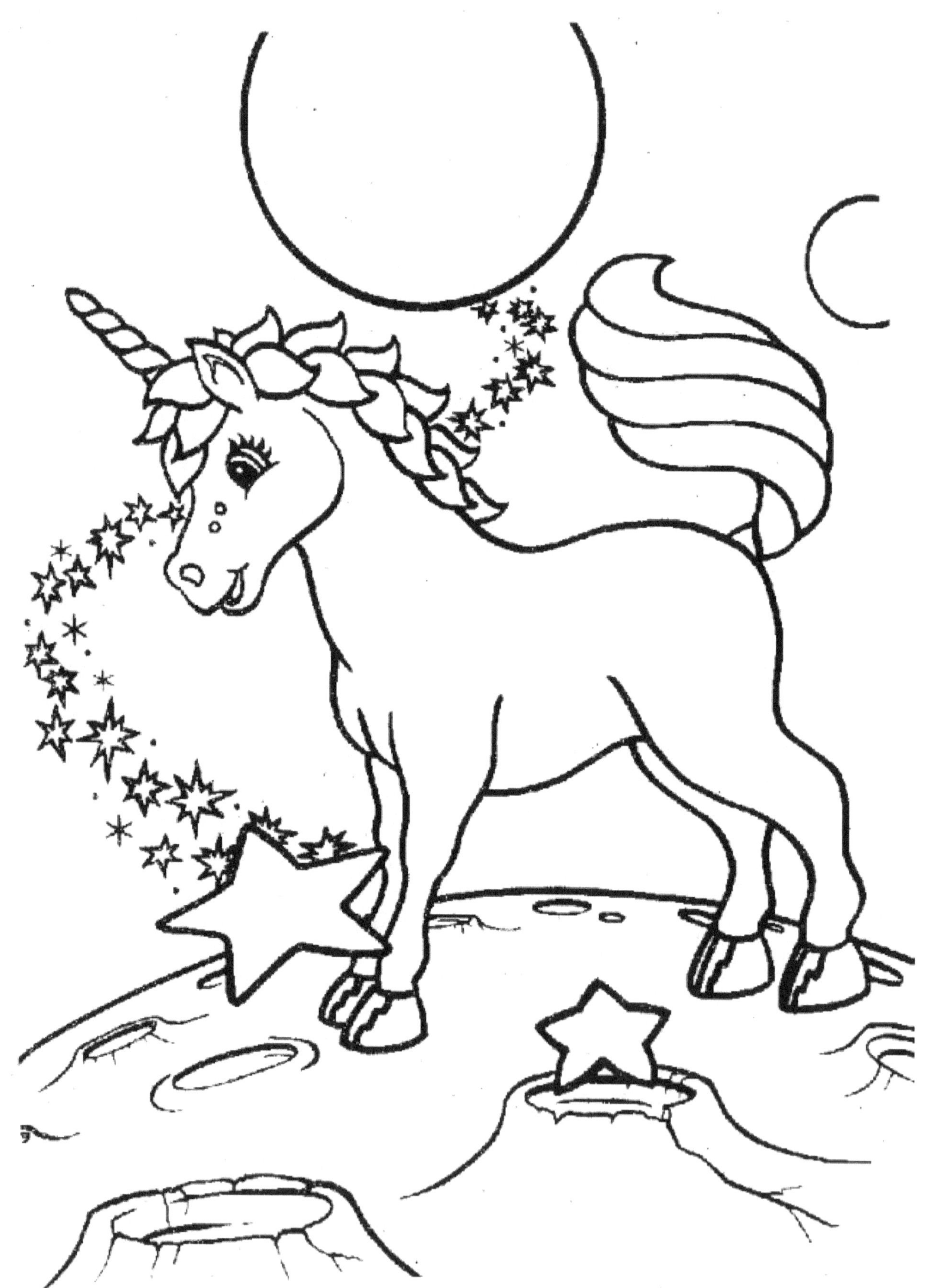

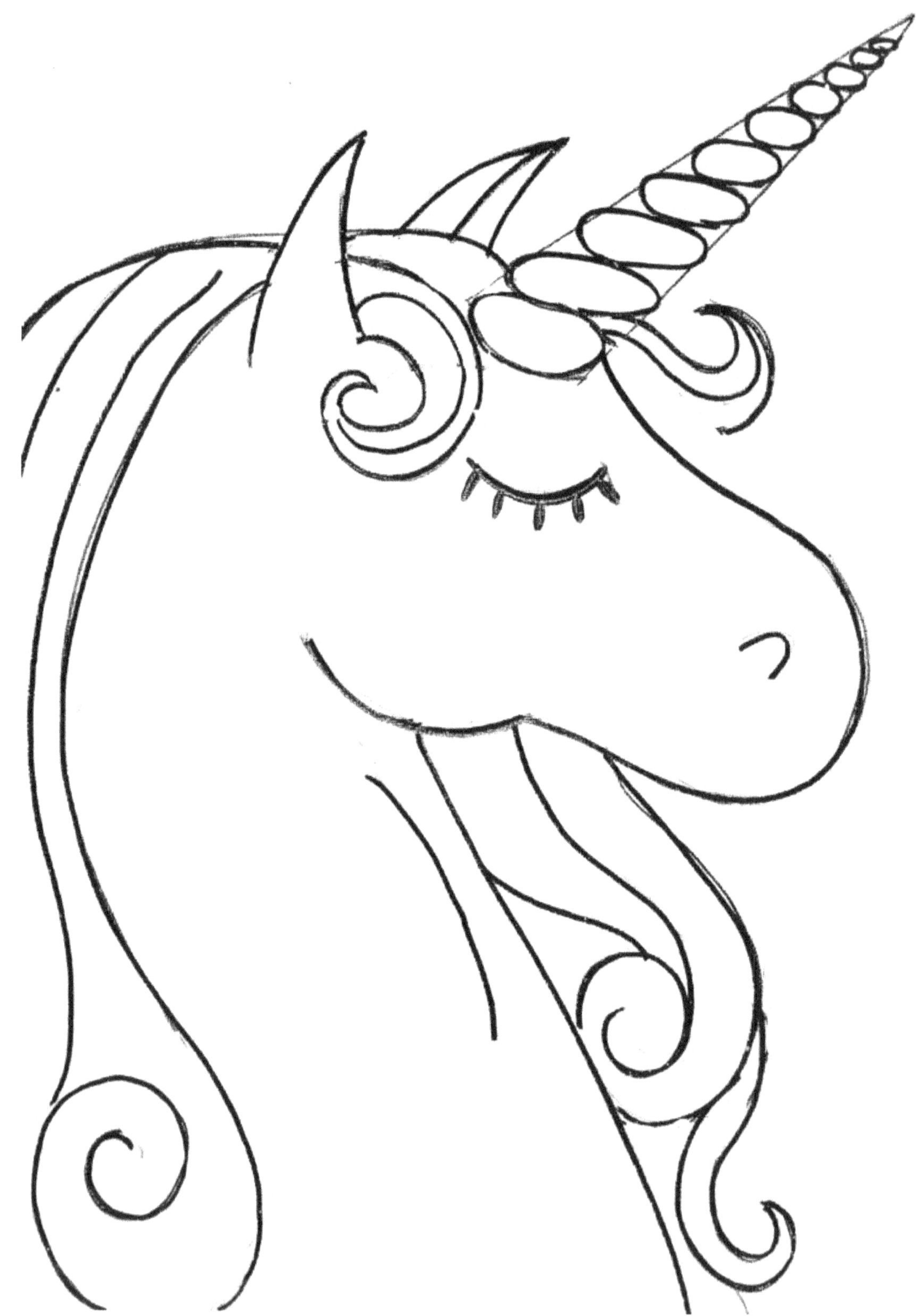

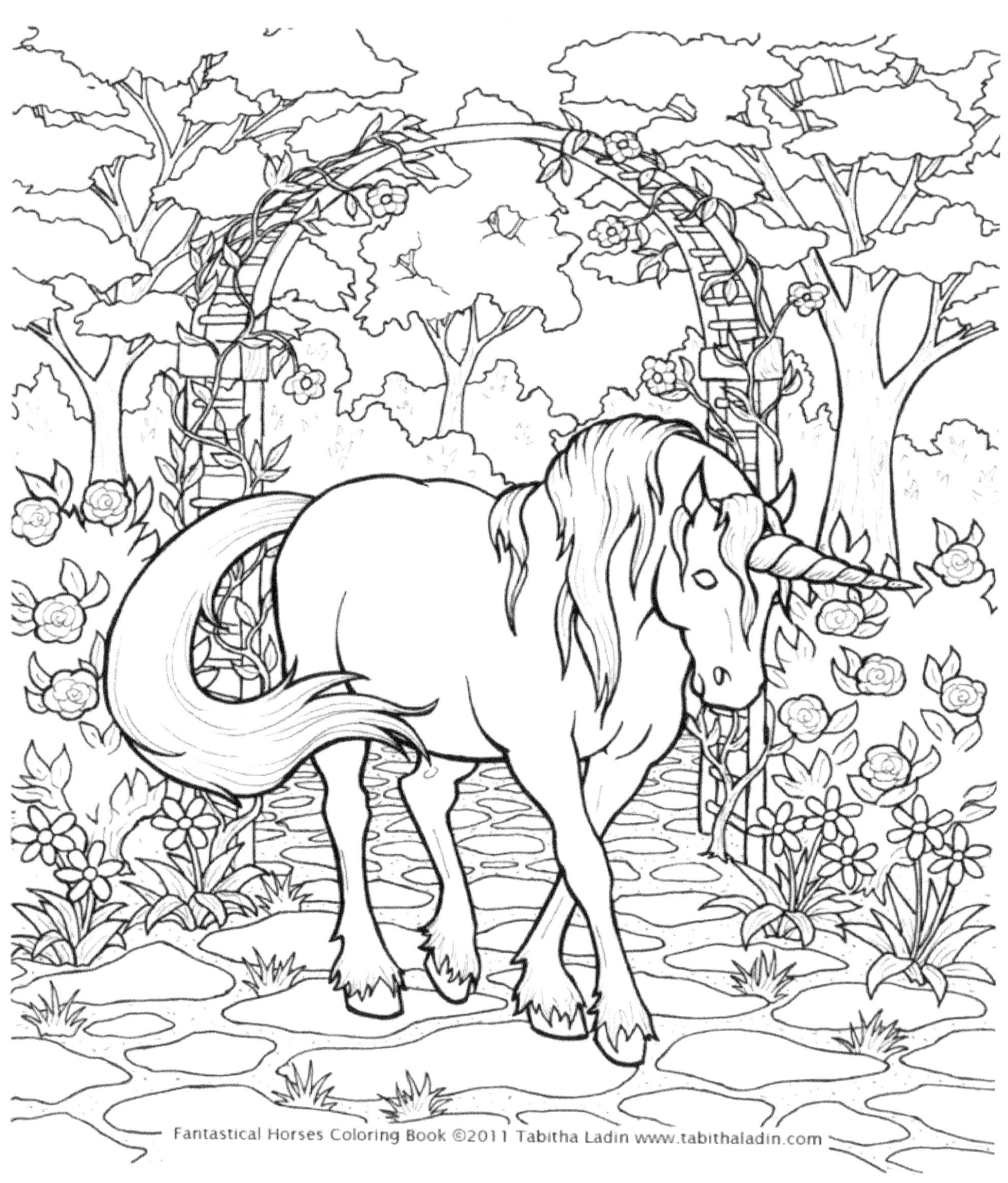

Fantastical Horses Coloring Book ©2011 Tabitha Ladin www.tabithaladin.com

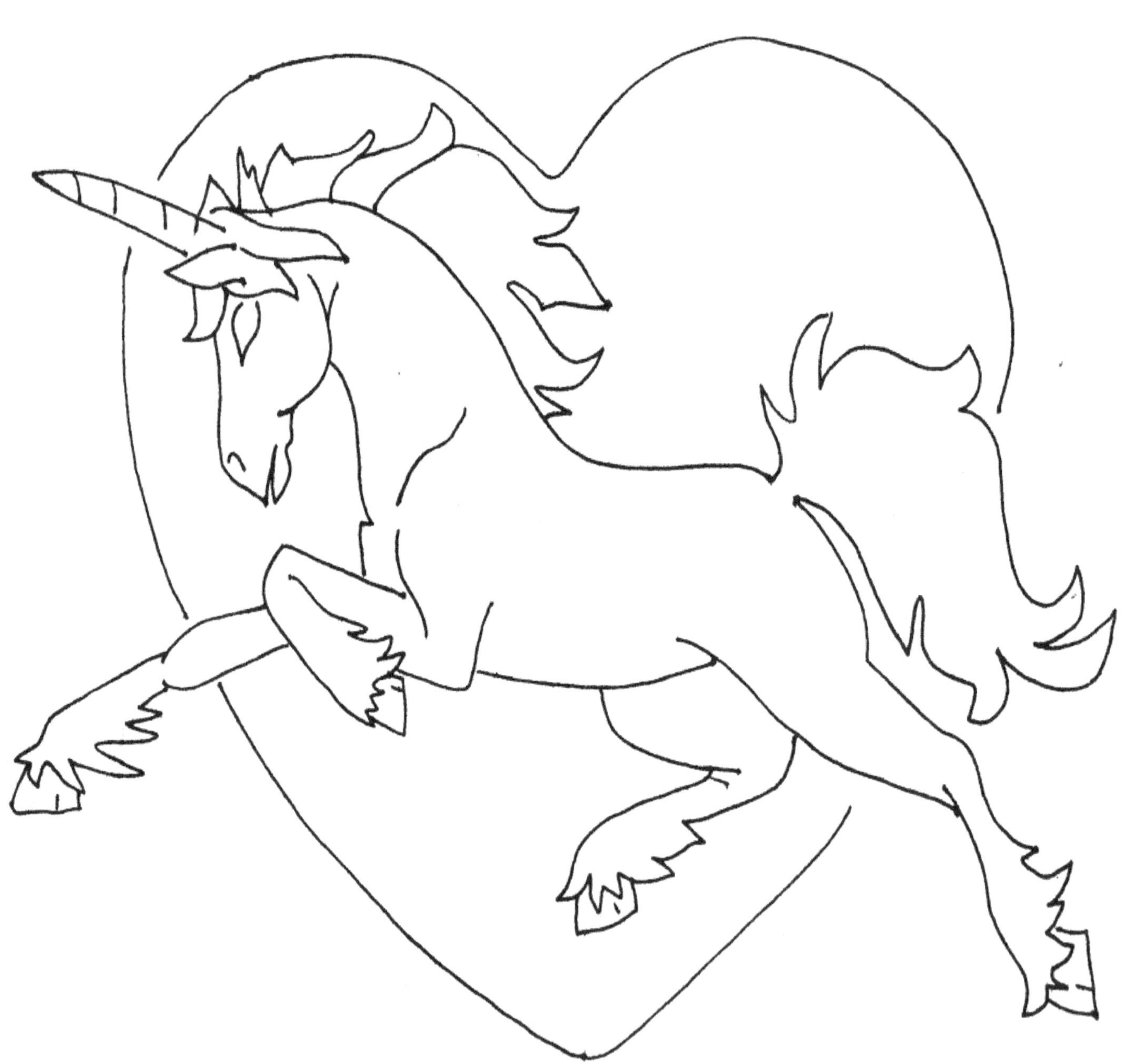

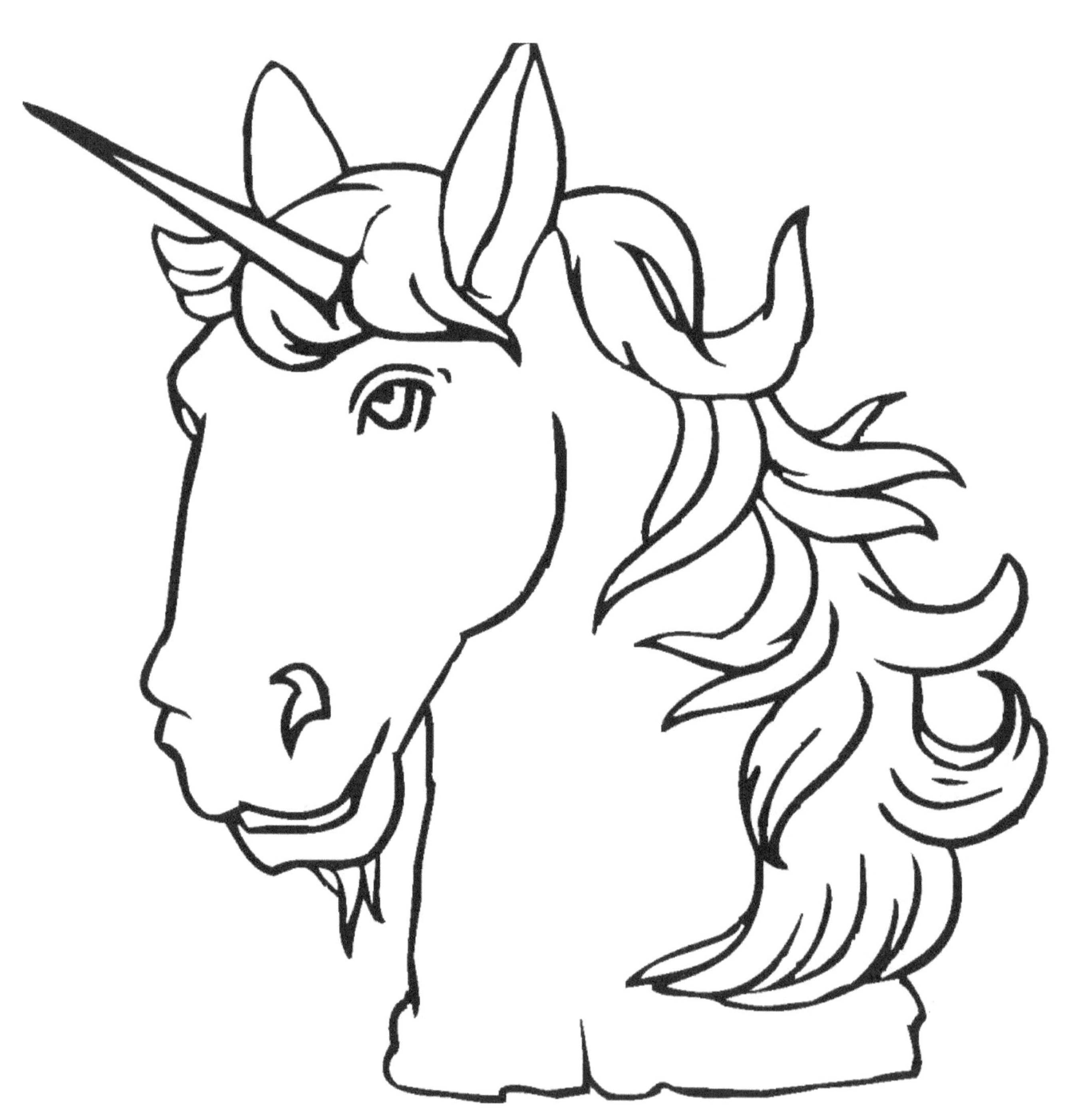

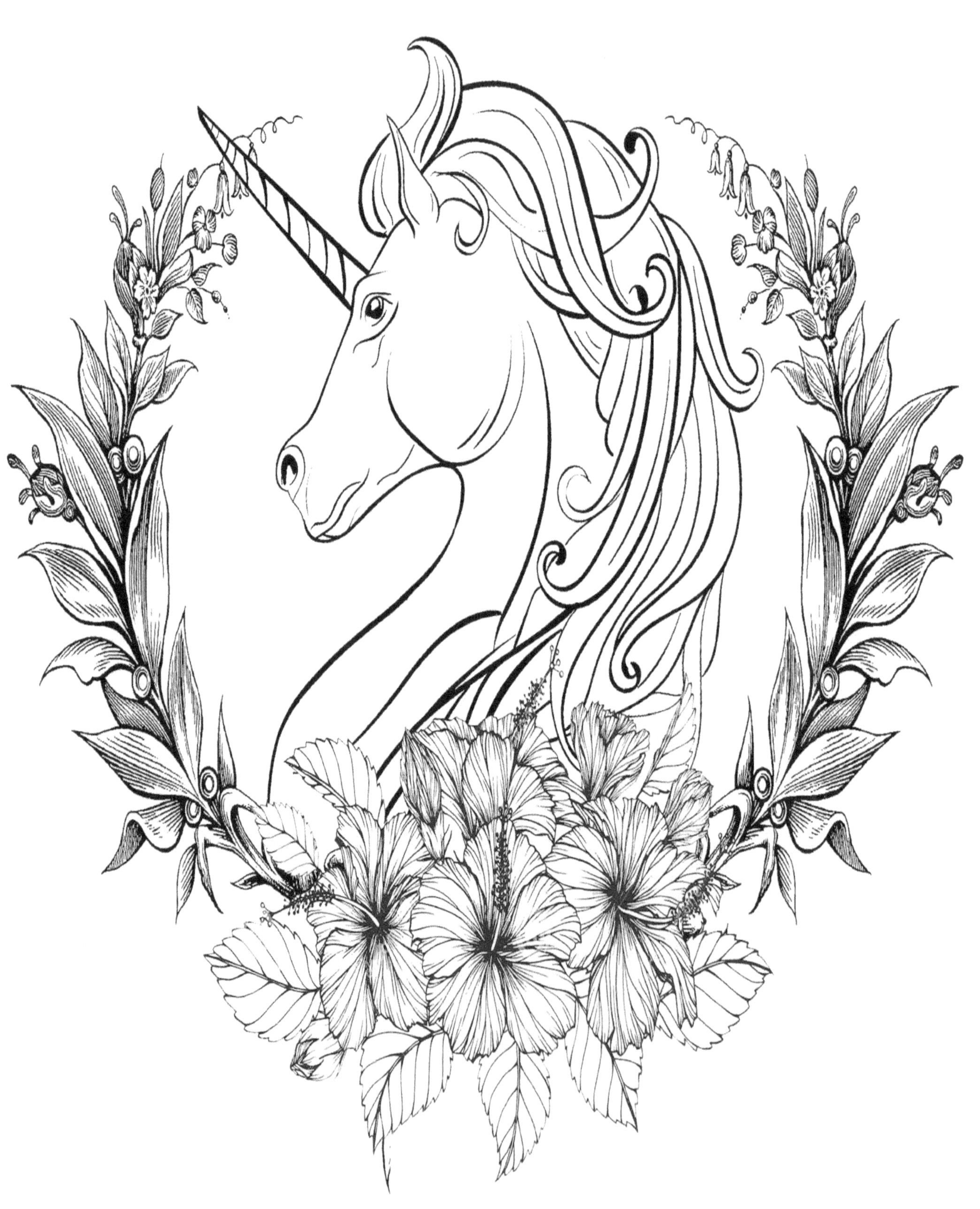

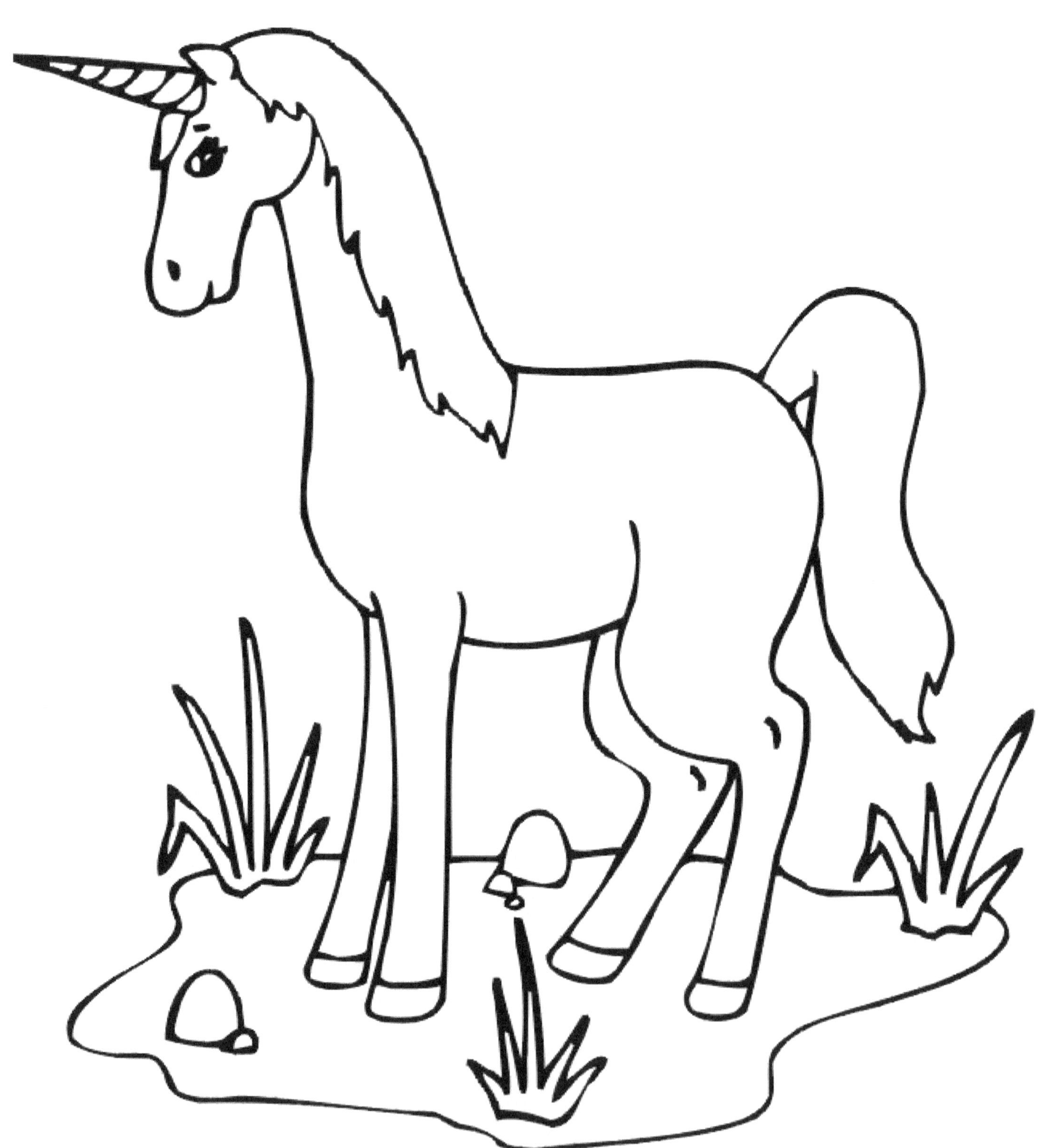

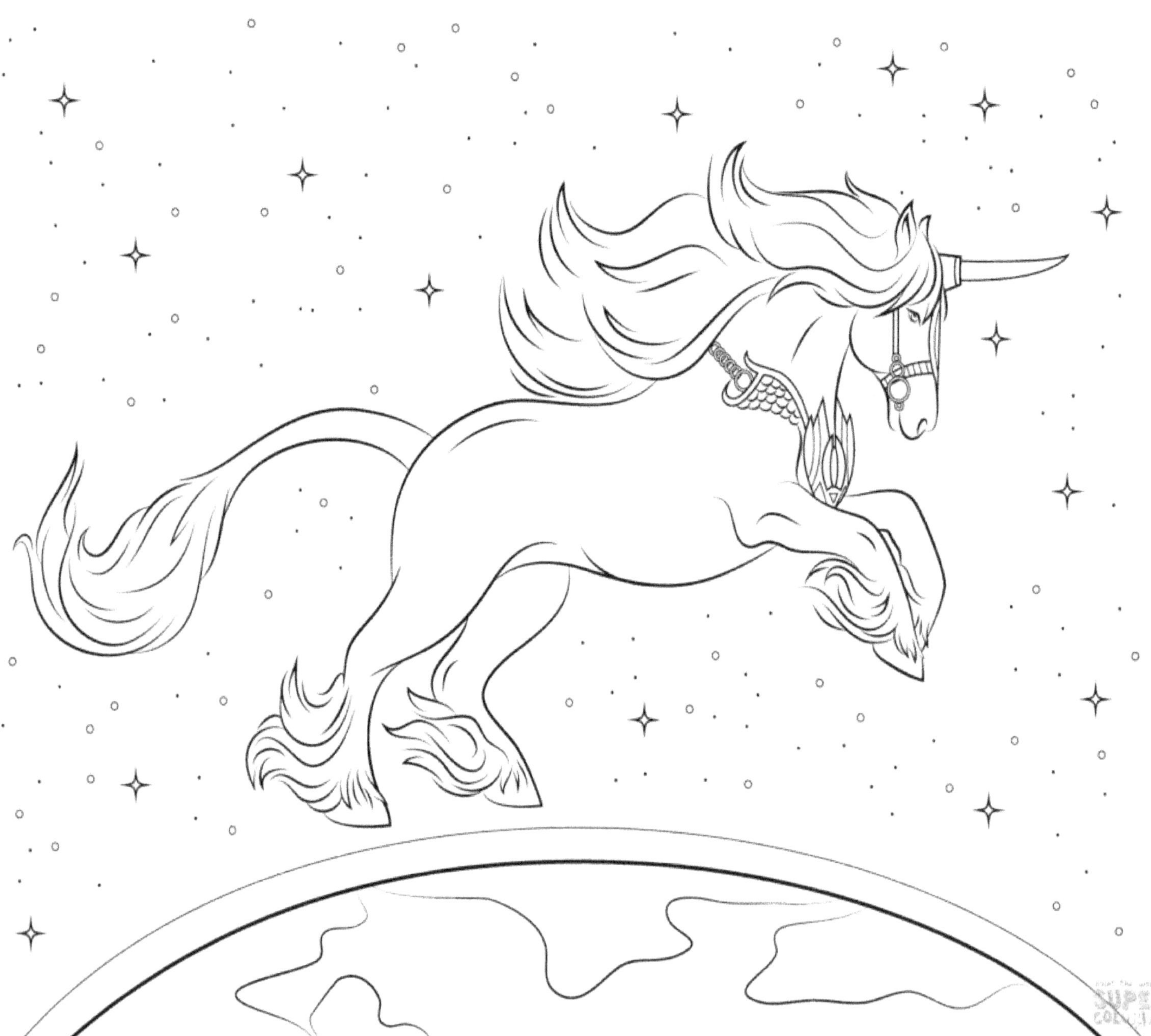

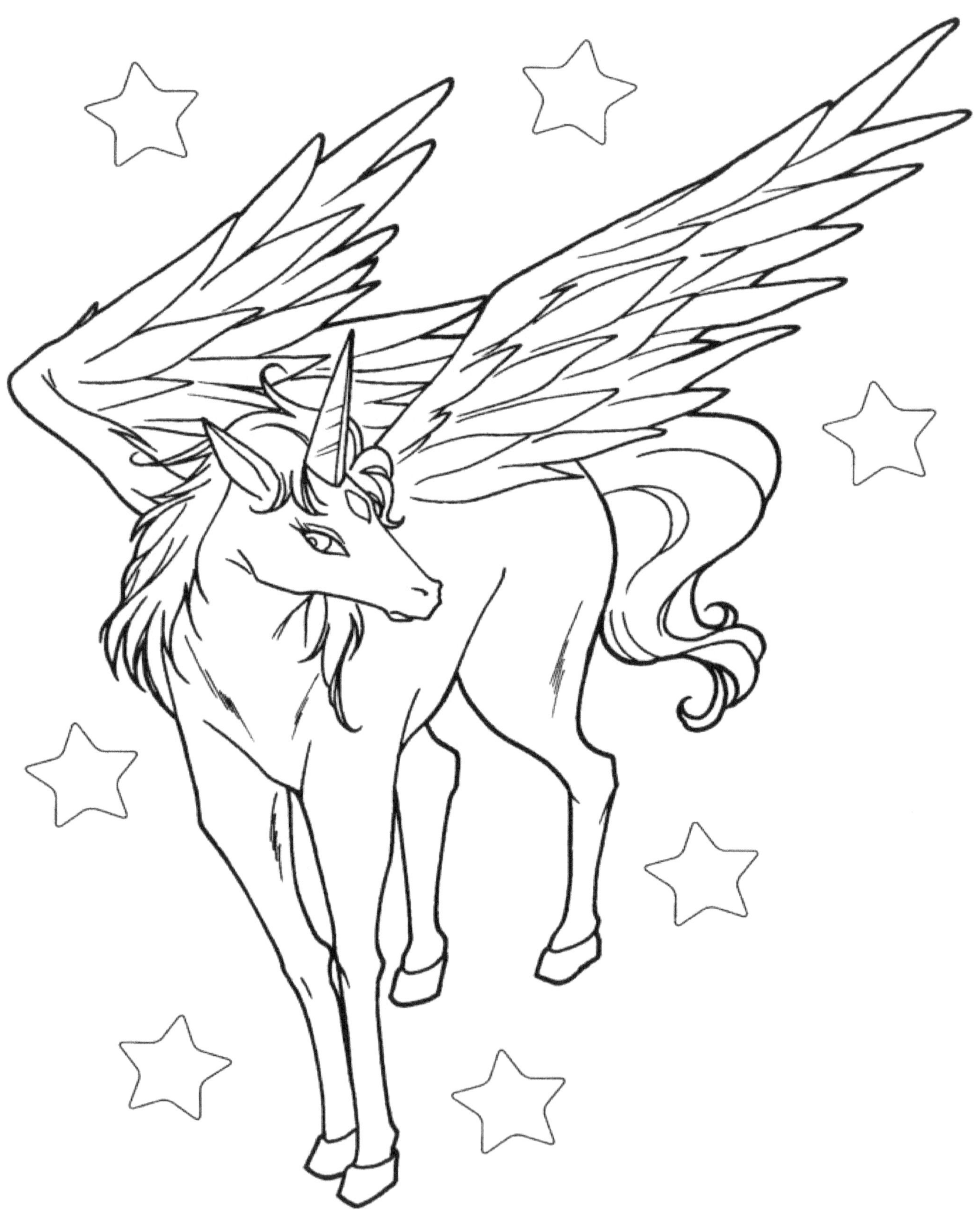

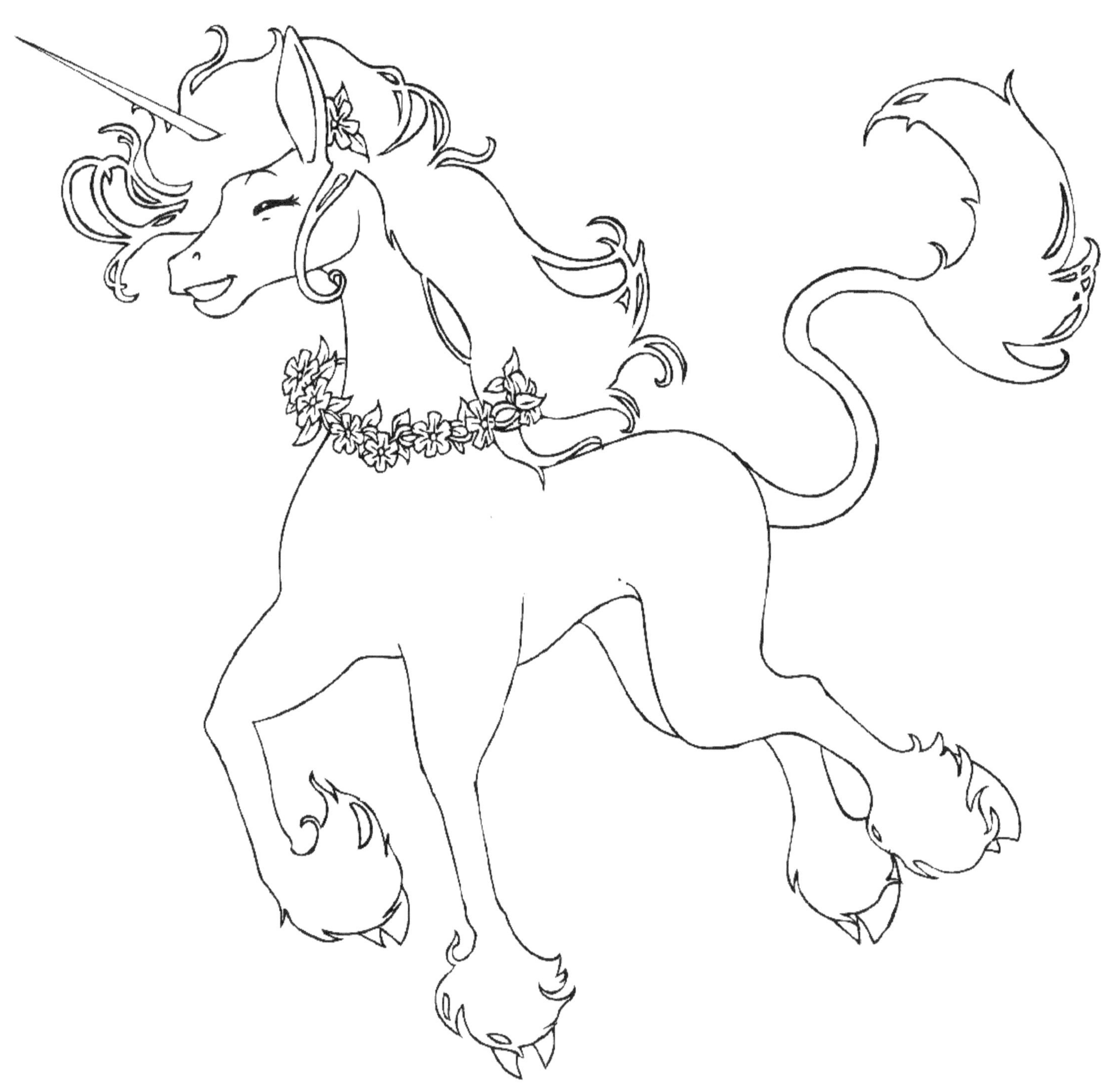

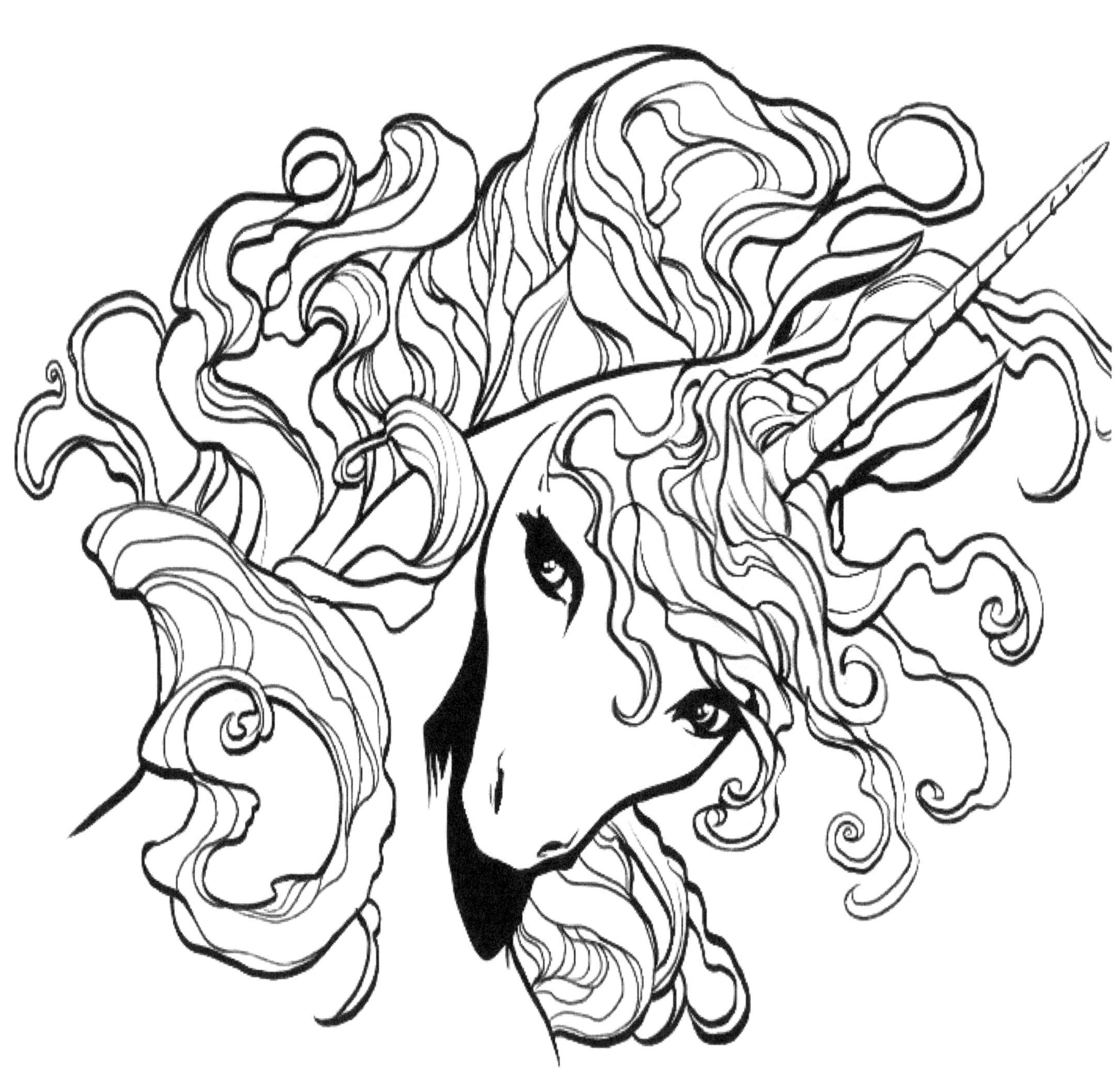

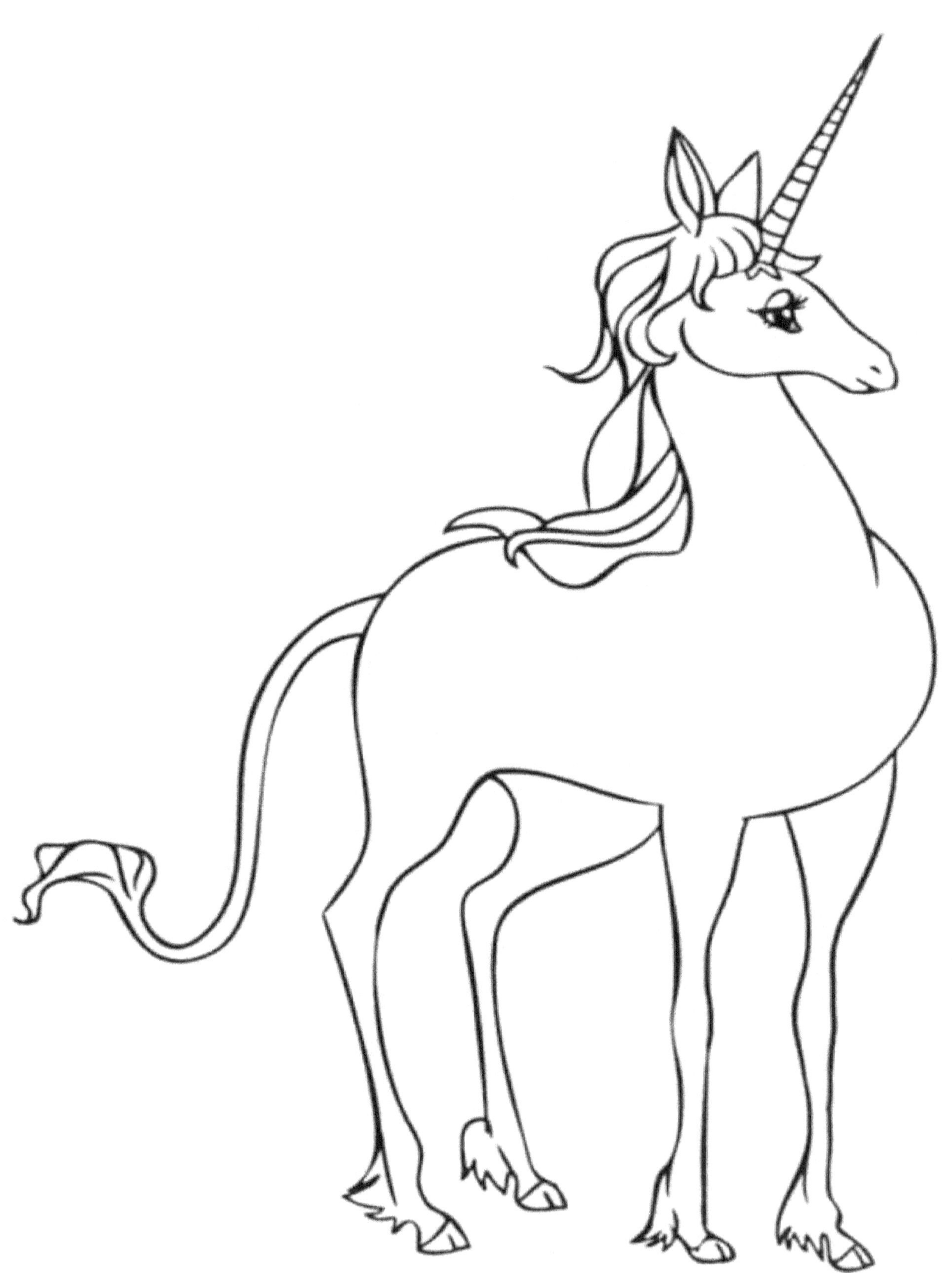

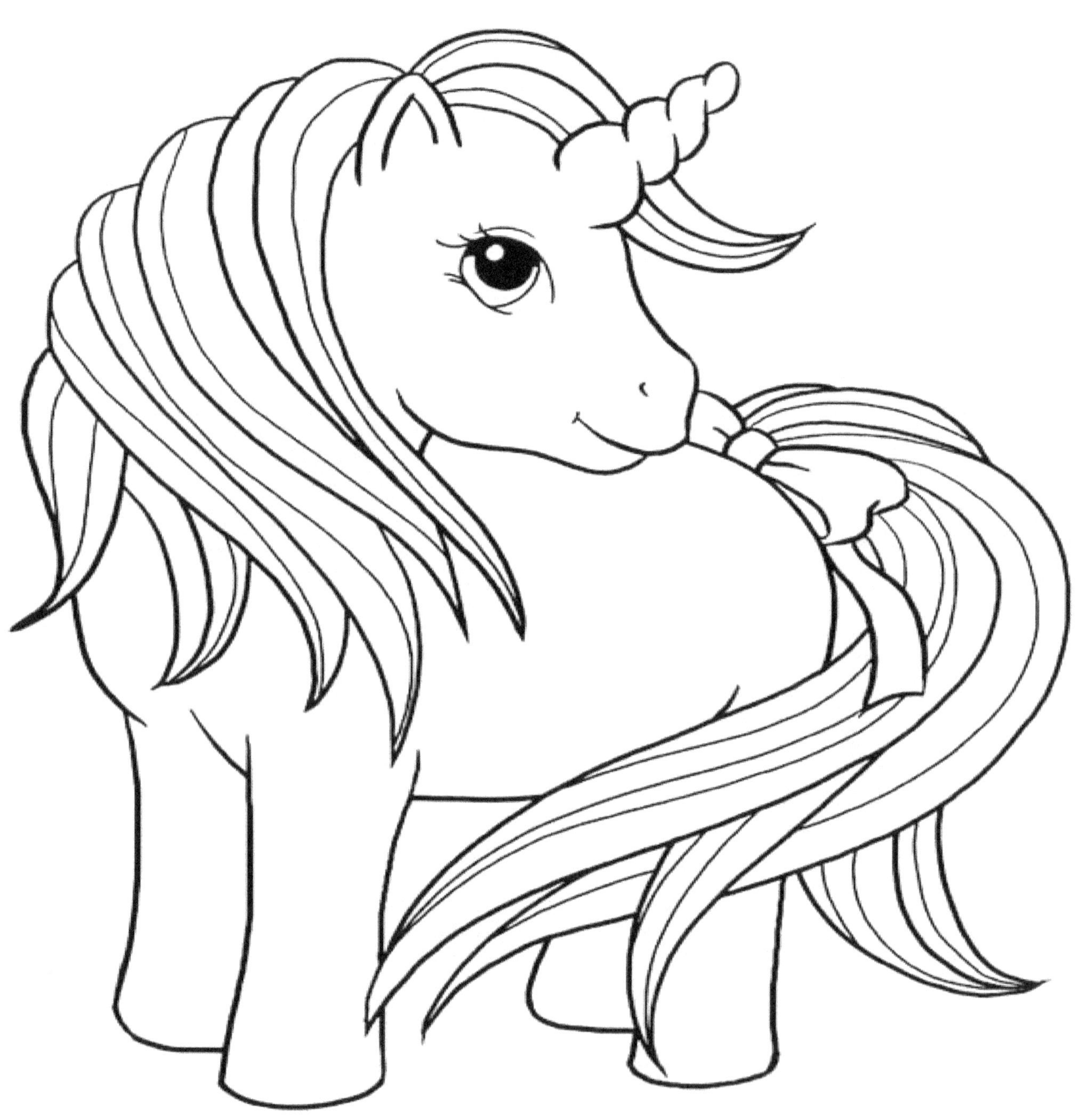

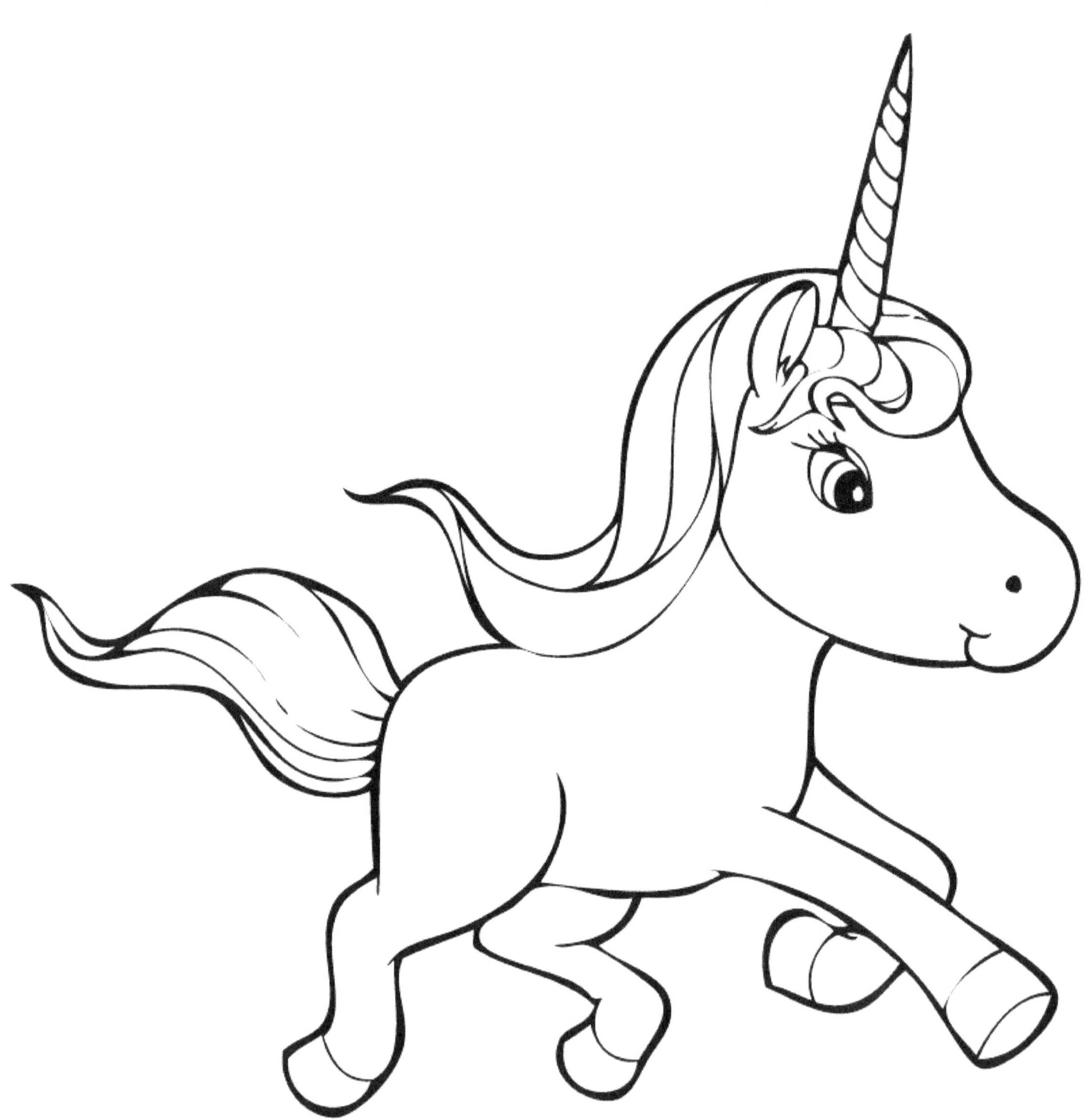

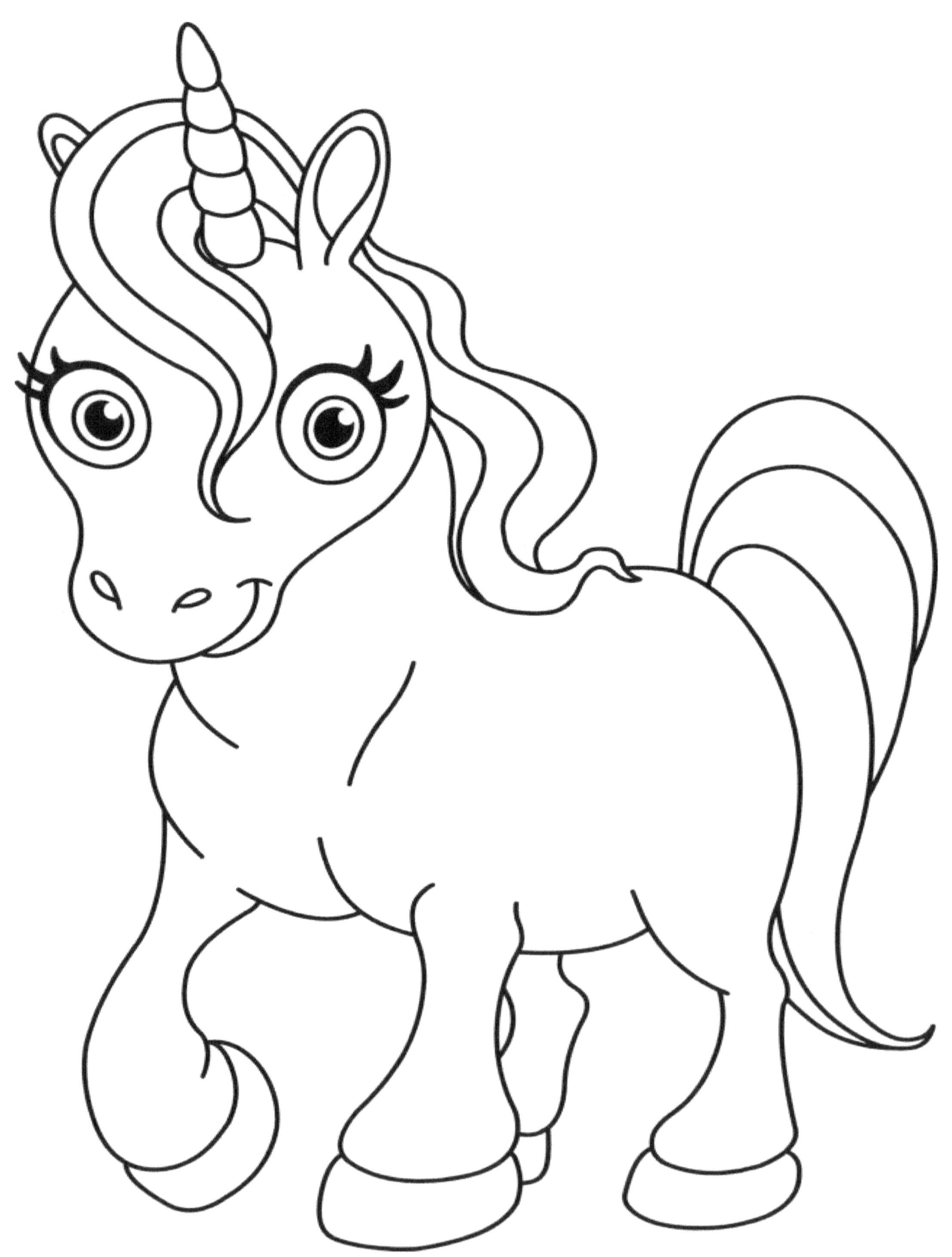

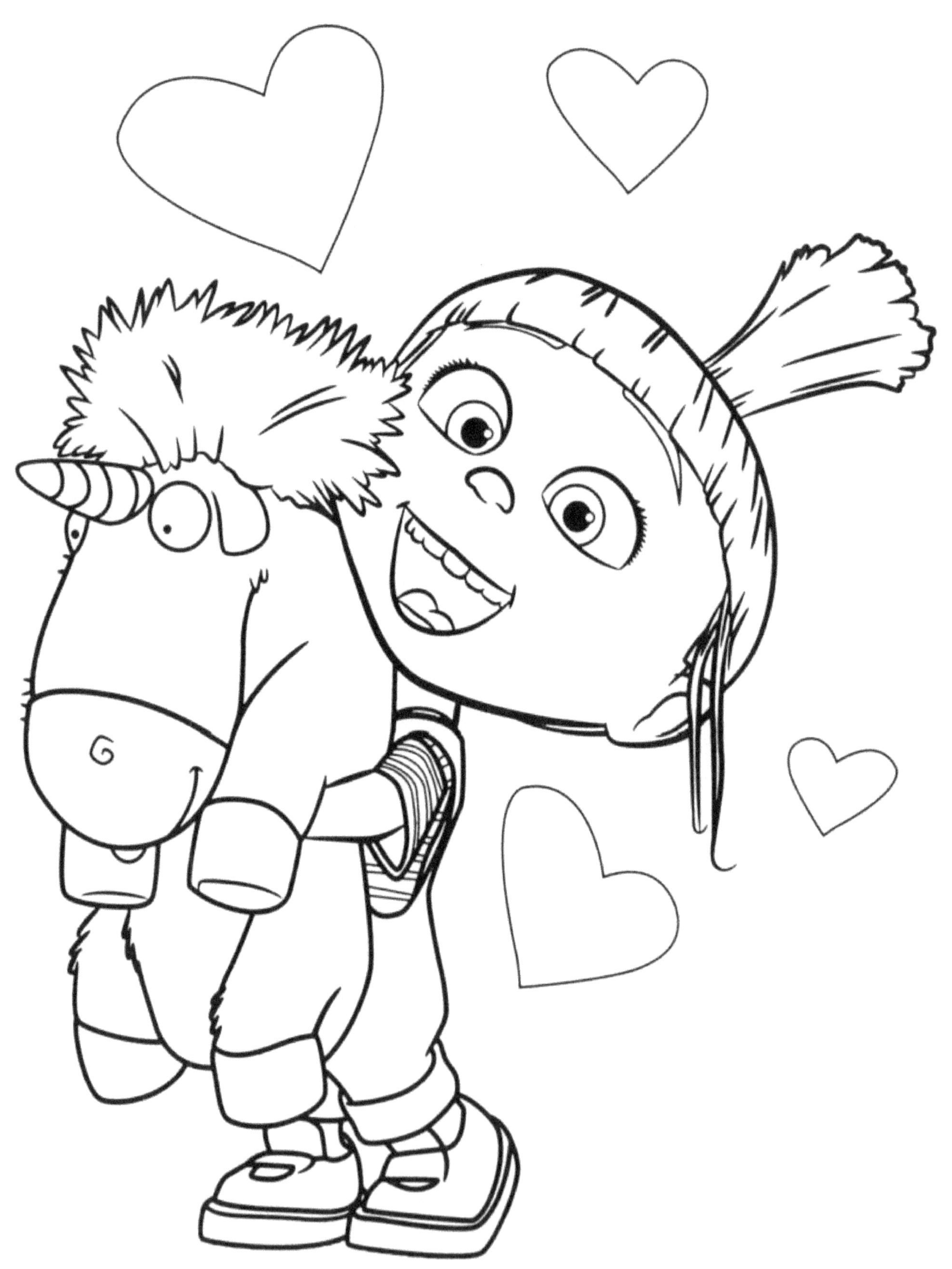

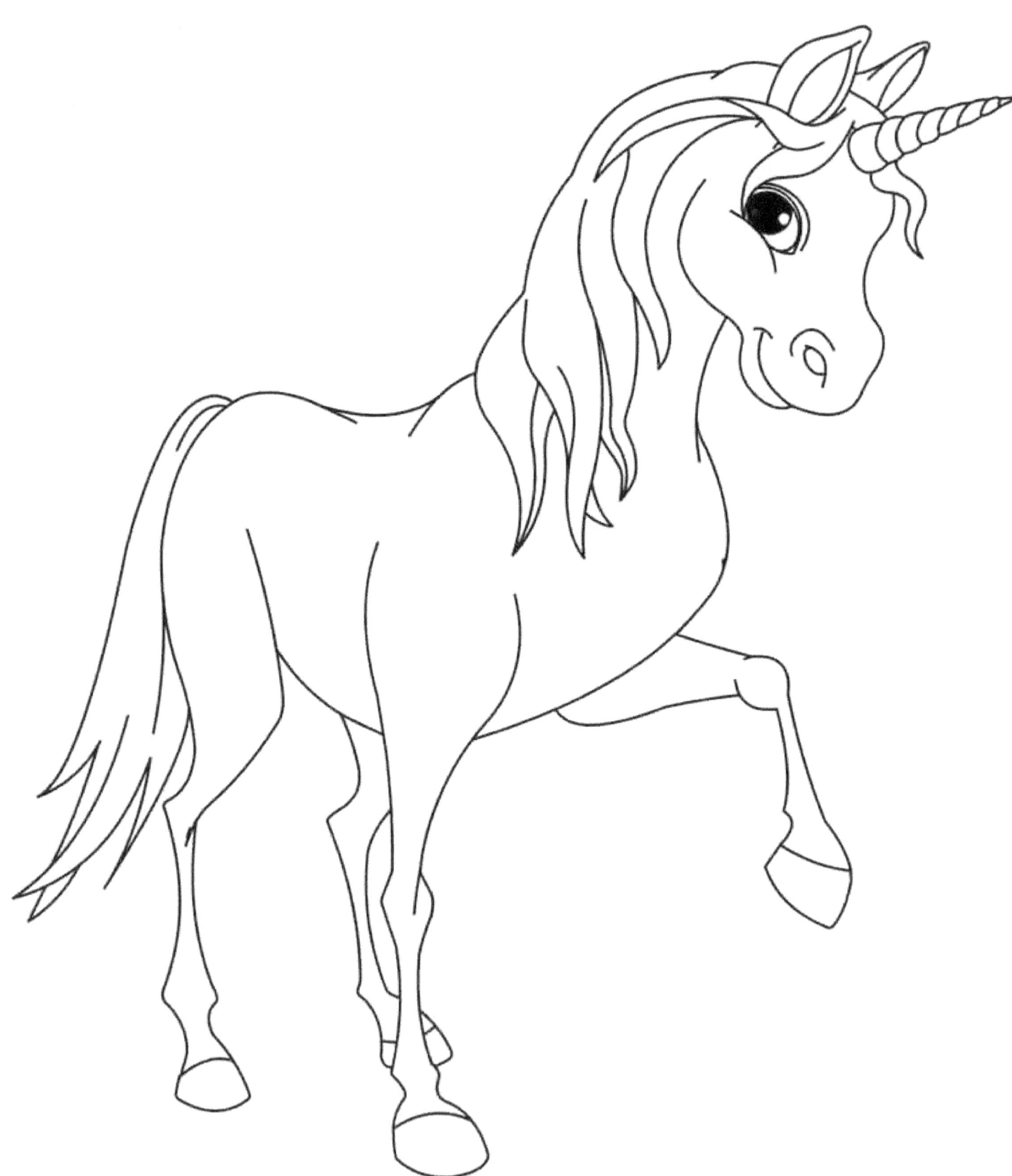

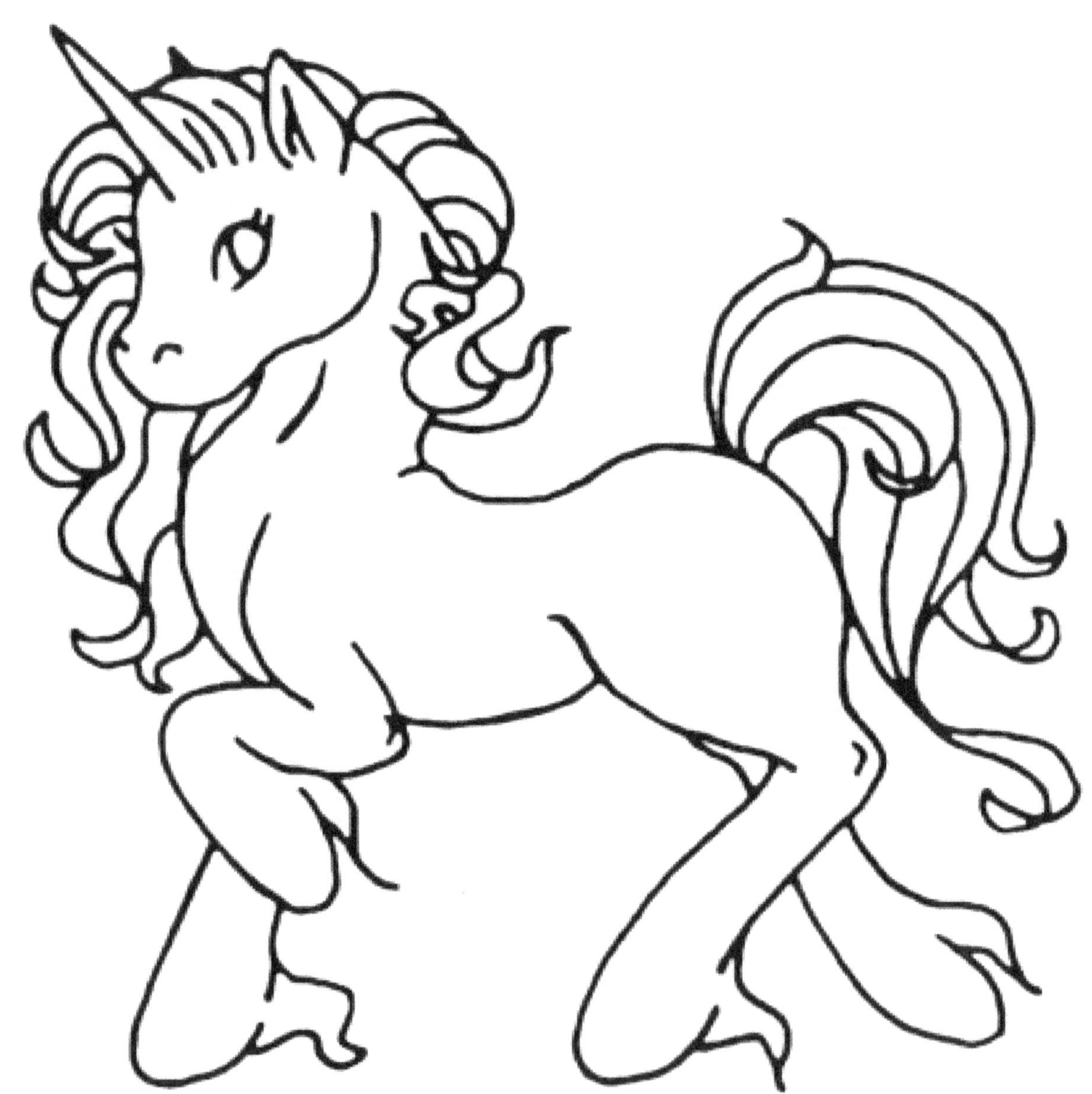